Reminiscences of

Sea Island Heritage

SANDLAPPER PUBLISHING, INC.
Orangeburg, South Carolina

Reminiscences of
Sea Island Heritage

by Ronald Daise

Sandlapper Publishing, Inc.
P.O. Box 730
Orangeburg, South Carolina 29116-0730

Photographs used by permission of Penn Community Services, Inc.
St. Helena Island, South Carolina. (Lifestyles of the Late 1800s to Early 1900s)

Photograph of "The Shout" (page 27) used by permission of
Mrs. Margaret M. Sanders.

Book design by Messagemakers.

First Edition, 1986
Second Edition, 1987

Fifth printing, 1998

Library of Congress Cataloging-in-Publication Data

Daise, Ronald
     Reminiscences of Sea Island Heritage.

     1. Afro-Americans — South Carolina — Saint Helena
Island — Social life and customs. 2. Saint Helena
Island (S.C.) — Social life and customs. I. Title.
F277.B3D35   1986   975.7'9900496073   85-26201
ISBN 0-87844-067-4 (hc)
ISBN 0-87844-081-X (second edition)
ISBN 0-87844-149-2 (pbk)

To Mama
for praying and remembering
and Natalie
for believing and keeping the faith alive

Acknowledgments

Immense gratitude to each person interviewed for this book. Also to: Emory S. Campbell, Executive Director of Penn Community Services, Inc., for allowing me to search for photographs; Penn Community Services, Inc., for granting permission to utilize the photographs; Mrs. Johnnie Mitchell, for making the right contacts; Ray and Elizabeth Ellis and Vern Williams, for offering helpful suggestions; Arthur R. Middleton, for sharing the typewriter; Edith F. Sumpter, Ann M. Perry, and Rev. Ervin Greene, for saying and singing the right things when my ears were attentive; the Department of Mass Media Arts at Hampton University, Hampton, Virginia, for training me to accomplish this endeavor; ultimately, to God, for working all things together in His own time.

Foreword

While reading the first printing of *Reminiscences of Sea Island Heritage,* the joy which characterized my visit to St. Helena Island in 1968 returned. To meditate on that ground consecrated by my forebears was a reverent and indelible experience. It was there that slaves were first freed after almost 250 years as chattels. Freedom was spontaneous and imposed, unanticipated and dramatic. Happily the transition was remarkably successful.

To write a foreword for the second edition of this book was a pleasure for three reasons: to commemorate the ingenuity, spirit, and resourcefulness of the slaves on St. Helena Island; to implant more deeply the revelations from my visit to the island; and to affirm my admiration for the humanism of Ronald Daise and his exemplary dedication to his rich Gullah heritage.

The Sea Islands, with which the Gullahs are identified, stretch along the coasts of South Carolina and Georgia. The Gullah dialect, with some variants, is spoken on all of the islands. A dialect variant on some of the Georgia islands is often called "Geechee," a word synonymous with Gullah. The consensus of scholars is that the term "Gullah" originated in West Africa, but how it came into usage is conjectural. The theories advanced thus far are as follows:

According to Professor Reed Smith,

> Both the word Gullah and the Negroes so named came from the West Coast of Africa, but exactly where has not been agreed upon. There are two widely held conjectures. One is that Gullah is a shortened form of Angola, the name of an African West Coast district lying south of the equator and the mouth of the Congo River. A small but positive bit of evidence to this effect is found in an entry of the Charleston City Council, under the year 1822, in which reference is made to "Gullah Jack" and his company of "Gullah or Angola Negroes." This indicates that, rightly or wrongly, as far back as 1822 the official governing body of the City of Charleston regarded Gullah as a corrupted form of Angola.
>
> A second, more probable suggestion is that Gullah comes from the name of the Liberian group of tribes known as the Golas living on the West Coast between Sierra Leone and the Ivory Coast. There Golas were formerly numerous and powerful, but have now dwindled to a small remnant tribe dwelling some thirty miles inland from Monrovia, the chief seaport of Liberia.[1]

According to John Bennett,

> The dialect of the West Coast, from which came these Gullah Negroes, was early commented upon as peculiarly harsh, quacking, flat in intonation, quick, clipped, and peculiar even in Africa. Bosman, the Dutch sailor, described its peculiar tonality and calls its speakers the "quaquas, because they gabbled

like geese."[2] [Author Ambrose E. Gonzalez noted that Bennett was a well-known writer of Charleston who gathered data about the Gullahs for twenty years.[3]]

An insight about the Gullahs from West Africa occurred in a study conducted in 1940 in Savannah, Georgia. When asked if he remembered any people brought over from Africa, an aged respondent replied,

> Yas, I know heaps ub um. Deah wuz "Golla" John Wiley, "Golla" Jim Bayfield — he wuz bought by Mahse Charles Lamar, and he sole im to Mr. McMullen. Den deah wuz "Golla" Jack, "Golla" Tom, "Golla" Silvie, "Golla" Charles Carr, "Golla" Bob, Chahlotte, Cain, and Jeanette, and "Golla" Alice. Dey wuz all bought by Mr. McMullen.

When asked the meaning of so many "Gollas," he replied,

> All duh people wut come from Africa aw obuhseas wuz call "Golla" and dey talk wuz call "Golla" talk.[4]

To questions regarding their utensils and tools, the old man answered,

> Dey would make any ting dey needed. Dey made spoons, trays, buckets. Dey made piggins an mawtah an pestle frum a lawg uh wood. Dey would make wooden cuttubs fuh meat and vegetubble and would dress some uh dem wid pretty figuhs.[5]

The term Gullah, meaning the dialect, indicates that it is spoken along the Guinea coast, an area extending from the Senegal River in West Africa to Angola and the Congo in central Africa. However, the people identified with the West Coast are usually referred to as "Guineas" or are called by the names of other countries. Aside from name and number, my objective is to present the Gullah people as historic characters, to track them from the Guinea coast to America, and to appraise and dignify their labor and achievements — apart from those of their slave masters. Their achievements are revealing and expand the dimensions of the Gullah heritage developed on the Sea Islands.

The odyssey began in 1434,[6] two centuries after European nations had agreed to cease enslaving one another.[7] The Portuguese could not resist the temptation to establish a slave trade of Africans, since that would not violate the European covenant nor be accountable to a government. From a limited scale to occasional shiploads of slaves, the trade grew in seventy years to several thousand persons annually. Spain and Portugal were the receiving countries. This chapter was just the beginning of the iniquitous business.

No doubt much about the Guinea slaves, which needs to be translated, could be found in the archives of Portugal and Spain. Fortunately a pertinent fragment is provided by Michael Cohn and Michael K.H. Platzer:

> Columbus also relied on Africans to reach America. His pilot, Pedro Alonso Nino, was a North African, and his cabin boy was listed as Diego El Negro. African slaves completed the crew lists of most of the early Portuguese and Spanish ships. Africans were reported to be good seamen and performed useful services off the coast of Africa for Europeans. [The home of Nino places him outside my focus on the Guinea slaves.]

The full significance of contributions by Guinea slaves is perceived in the context of the maritime status of countries in the fifteenth and sixteenth centuries:

> ... the tiny country of Portugal was one of the great empires in the world because of its shipping.[9]

> The Spanish empire supported the Spanish fleet on all seas of the world and grew to sudden wealth and prosperity.[10]

At the time, maritime commerce was the largest and most prestigious government-sponsored operation in the two countries. Voyages were hazardous, of course, but were it not for the demonstrated superior seamanship of the Guinea slaves, there can be no doubt that sailors native to the two countries would have been preferred. The paradoxical domination of Guinea slaves in the crew lists was indeed an achievement. It can also be assumed that the collateral effect of this development was to stimulate the Guineas' sense of worth and inspire mental growth.

Another maritime achievement is the share of credit attributable to the crew which made it possible to discover America. Though unsung, the Guineas irrefutably were active participants in the monumental historic discovery of the new world. Their next achievement was their support in its development.

When Columbus discovered America in 1492, under sponsorship of the Queen of Spain, he and his successors formed a settlement on the island they named Santo Domingo, now shared by the Dominican Republic and Haiti. The island's Indian population, estimated at a million, was enslaved. By 1514 only fourteen thousand had survived the hard, unaccustomed labor of mining for gold, the cruelties inflicted upon them, and the toll of new diseases.[11]

As early as 1503, a few Guineas had been brought to Santo Domingo, and it was found that each one did as much work as four Indians, that they thrived and multiplied rapidly. Shipload after shipload of them were soon brought to

xi

the island. In 1510 King Charles V granted exclusive rights to one company to import four thousand slaves and establish regular traffic between the Guinea coast and what was now his colony. Importation and the birth rate were so high that shortly there was a Guinea for every Spaniard in the colony. In whatever direction the Spaniards took during their career of conquest, the Guineas went with them.[12]

After the arrival of the Guineas, the true source of Santo Domingo's wealth was found to be in cultivation of its soil, not digging for gold. Sugar cane was introduced, intensively cultivated, and yielded a handsome profit.[13] The labor of the Guineas gives them the undeniable distinction as the first farmers and producers of capital in the new world. To grow sugar cane the Guineas and Indians were worked beyond reasonable bounds. The Indians died and the Guineas revolted. By then, however, Santo Domingo was no longer important to Spain; her attention was concentrated on the mainland which is now the United States.[14]

St. Augustine, Florida, became the Spanish military headquarters in North America, and Guinea slaves were brought there in the late 1500s as property of the king. In the first hospital in the United States, built there in 1597, a Guinea woman attended patients, including Guineas and Indians.[15]

It can be assumed that ships which made the voyages to the mainland customarily had crews that were predominantly Guinean, but two new achievements arise in assessing this phase of the Guineas' experience: 1) the first revolt of record in the new world, an example of courage and expression of manhood unyielding to harsh treatment; and 2) inclusion in the discovery of St. Augustine in the expedition of 1528[16] and the founding of the city—the oldest in the United States—in 1565.

After witnessing a century of Spain's profitable labor by Guinea slaves, England entered the slave trade in 1562, followed by the Dutch, French, and Danes. They secured colonies in the West Indies that prospered by producing sugar cane. Agriculture required more slaves than the Guinea coast could furnish, and the interior of central Africa became the primary area of supply. This development complicated tracking of the Guineas except in instances in which they are specifically mentioned. Two such occasions have been noted, and others may be found in the history of the West Indies.

T. J. Woofter, Jr., states in his book that Africans were introduced as slaves on St. Helena Island shortly after the English occupation in 1711 and that Gambia and Guiney Negroes were the favorite slaves.[17] Duncan Clinch Heyward finds that before the Civil War 90 percent of the Negroes on the Combahee plantation were Gullahs, as was the case on every rice plantation in South Carolina and Georgia as well as the sea islands of those states.[18]

It is my hope that readers share my enlightenment about achievements of the Gullah-speaking people. My research for this foreword suggests that it is only a fraction of the information which might be gathered for a fuller account of the historical roots of the Gullah phenomena and the Gullah speech, the oldest Anglo-American dialect spoken in this country.[19]

Clarence L. Holte

New York
July, 1987

Sources

1. Guy B. Johnson, *Folk Culture on St. Helena Island, South Carolina* (Chapel Hill: University of North Carolina Press, First Edition, 1930), 4.

2. Ibid, 5.

3. Ambrose E. Gonzalez, *The Black Border: Gullah Stories of the Carolina Coast* (Columbia, S.C.: State Press, 2nd printing, 1922), 9.

4. WPA, Georgia Writers Project, Savannah Unit, *Drums and Shadows: Survival Studies among Georgia Coastal Negroes* (Athens: University of Georgia Press, 1986), 66.

5. Ibid, 67.

6. W. O. Blake, comp.; *The History of Slavery and the Slave Trade* (Columbus, Ohio: J. & H. Miller, 1858), 95.

7. Ibid, 22.

8. Michael Cohn and Michael K. H. Platzer, *Black Men of the Sea* (New York: Dodd & Company, 1978), 3, 4.

9. Columbia Encyclopedia, 20th printing, 1947, 1429.

10. Ibid, 1664.

11. Blake, *The History of Slavery*, 96.

12. Samuel Hazard, *Santo Domingo, Past and Present with a Glance at Hayti* (New York: Harper & Bros., 1873), 45.

13. Blake, *The History of Slavery*, 96, 253.

14. Ibid, 254.

15. WPA, Federal Writers Project, State of Florida, *Florida: A Guide to the Southernmost State* (New York: Oxford University Press, 1939), 241.

16. Sir Arthur Helps, *The Spanish Conquest in America* (London: John Lane, 1904), 294.

17. T. J. Woofter, Jr., *Black Yeomanry: Life on St. Helena Island* (New York: Henry Holt and Company, 1930), 17, 22.

18. Duncan Clinch Heyward, *Seed from Madagascar* (Chapel Hill: University of North Carolina Press, 1937), 160.

19. Frank J. Clingberg, *An Appraisal of the Negro in Colonial South Carolina* (Washington, D.C.: Associated Publishers, 1941), 20.

Preface

Sea Island culture is in transition. Even since my birth in 1956, some aspects of it have died out completely; others linger, but falteringly. As a consequence of change, old tales —

> . . . The coachwhip was a notorious viper. Not only was it venomous, it took painstaking efforts to ensure its victims had died. After striking someone, it stuck its head into his nostrils. If the victim was still breathing, the coachwhip would coil its lengthy body around him and, with his tail, whip him to death!

old spirituals —

> . . . Heah come Sista Mary,
> Comin' witha broom in her han'.
> Sweep, Sista Mary. Keep sweepin'.
> Sweep clean the way to the Promise' Lan'.
>
> I kno' I got religion. So glad!
> An' the worl' can't do me no ha'm!

old beliefs —

> . . . Children born with a caul, the filmy fetal membrane covering the head, were thought to have special powers. The sick were brought to these infants to be touched and, consequently, healed. Such children, according to belief, also could see visions.

and old customs —

> . . . To assure that an unwanted guest would not revisit his home, the host would throw salt over his shoulder as the individual departed.

soon may be nonexistent.

Change is inevitable and necessary, yes. And some traditions should be extinguished. But picture albums, scrap books and tape recordings of a heritage should be maintained so that heritage will live not only in the memories of a proud and aged group of Sea Island blacks. St. Helena Island heritage mirrors that of neighboring Sea Island communities, yet remains a largely unsung chapter of Americana.

The history usually told (and told through the eyes of those who are not native to the area) encompasses these facts:

Spanish explorer Lucas Vasquez de Allyon discovered St. Helena Island in 1520, naming it in honor of his patron saint, Santa Elena, the mother of the first Christian Roman emperor, Constantine. The land had been named Chicora by the native Indian tribe. In addition to the Chicora, other Indian tribes included the Catawbas, Muscogees and Cherokees. The eighteen by four- to seven-mile island (located off southeastern South Carolina between Charleston and Savannah, Georgia) became an English possession in 1763. With agriculture as the chief occupation, chattel slavery was soon introduced to promote the cultivation of corn, indigo and, chiefly, Sea Island cotton.

A large percentage of black slaves brought to labor on the large Sea Island plantations were from West Africa. Isolated by the waterways, they cleaved to the culture of their motherland.

Following the capture of St. Helena and the surrounding Sea Islands by Union troops during the Civil War, about 10,000 black inhabitants remained on the land deserted by the plantation owners and their families. The newly freed slaves, along with carpetbaggers, subsequently bought small farm plots of land, which had been confiscated for taxes. The white population steadied at about fifty residents for many years. The isolation of the island fostered a people with a unique language, Gullah, and a unique heritage, which includes being the source of the Union's first all-black regiment, organized in 1862.

The history of this people is more than an embodiment of facts. Their own stories are colorful, peculiar, provocative and worthy of being told.

Mrs. Agnes C. Sherman, curator of the Y. W. Bailey Cultural Center at Penn Community Services, Inc., asserts: "Black history really began here on St. Helena Island. We were the first freedmen. We had the first school (Penn Normal, Industrial and Agricultural School, established in 1862). And we were the first landowners: we were never sharecroppers."

Reflecting this zeal, *Reminiscences of Sea Island Heritage* is an aesthetic documentation of the lifestyles, customs, superstitions and lore of the St. Helena Island people, which soon may be altogether forgotten. As condominiums and resort communities become as commonplace as the Spanish moss draping aged oaks, and as third and fourth generation Islanders cease to identify with a heritage dear to their forbears, that heritage is being hushed and stilled. This work is a time capsule, presented with Sea Island flavoring. It is a people's story of how they "got over," by surviving the hard times, and how and what they learned about life.

The photographs, housed in the Y. W. Bailey Cultural Center, span the late 1800s through early 1900s.

Forgotten Moments

Only few remember.
A history of a people has been hushed, been stilled—
Yet only few weep.
Only few sing the old songs
Or recall precious moments.
Time, progress and shortsightedness are silencing a heritage!
Precious memories, though,
Are like the lyrics of old slave songs.
They should not be
Stored up
In the minds of
A few.
They should linger—
From generation to generation—
Lending meaning to the past,
Nurturing strength and hope
For the future.

—Ronald Daise

Only few remember.

Wash basins, water pitchers and bed chambers were necessary during the period of outdoor privies and no indoor plumbing.

In a typical Island kitchen of the early 1900s, wood stoves were used for cooking and heating; kerosene lamps, for lighting.

Pots were hung on the kitchen walls for storage before the introduction of cabinets.

One-roomed, patched-roofed houses were commonplace during the early 1900s.

Despite primitive living conditions, the Islanders maintained a quiet dignity, as exemplified by this gentleman posing proudly beside his home.

This Island home probably was destroyed during a hurricane or storm. A handpump (for water) and a homemade board washtub are pictured.

The buckboard, a horse-driven carriage, was used by Islanders. Oxen carts, horse and buggies, horseback and bateaux provided other modes of transportation.

A group of women are ferried in a bateau. Because bridges were not constructed until the mid-1900s, the isolated Islanders maintained many traditions and superstitions brought from Africa and borne during slavery.

These Island boys ride upon one of the first cars driven on St. Helena Island's dirt roads.

The waterways were easily accessible to all for transporting, fishing, crabbing, shrimping and picking oysters.

To school, to church, to prayer services, the Islanders walked the dirt and shelled roads. Prayer houses were located on each plantation (or community). Islanders journeyed to prayer meetings on Sundays, Tuesdays and Thursdays. Assembling at dusk, they congregated in the small buildings, worshipping for an hour to an hour-and-a-half. The service ended with members doing the "Shout," a dance of praise.

This driver steers his oxen cart in front of Brick Baptist Church, the oldest church for blacks on the Island. Built in 1855, the building still houses the original pews and interior fixtures constructed by slaves.

Manufactured dolls were a rarity. Ones made from corn shucks were more common.

Checkers, a favored pastime, is enjoyed by a group of instructors.

Children's activities included ring games, such as "Sally over the Water" and "Go in and out the Window."

Community and school bands delighted many during Island celebrations such as the Emancipation Day Parade on January 1. The event commemorated the signing of the Declaration of Independence.

Farmer's Fair, once an annual event, was highlighted with a barbecue cooked in a big iron pot.

Spanish moss draped from the trees makes this dirt road picturesque. The Island was first named Chicora after its native Indian tribe. Bordering islands still bear Indian names: Dathaw (now Dataw), Wassaw (now Warsaw), Coosaw and Polawanna.

"Peace and plenty is in that land where I'm bound, where I'm bound."

A visit to Margaret M. Sanders' Frogmore Manor Plantation leads travelers beyond moss-bearded oaks. If those venerable oaks could speak, they would expound on St. Helena Island's history.

They would tell of a time when plantations stretched hundreds of acres and teemed with Negro slaves farming cotton, rice and indigo. They would bemoan the sultry summertime and its accompanying humiliations: mosquitoes, sand flies and plagues of smallpox. Too, they would boast of resplendent greenery and grandiose sunsets that colorfully decorate the coastal marshes and beachfronts.

After directing you down the long, narrow dirt road, those oaks would point to Frogmore Manor, a relic of southern plantation lifestyle. The twelve-roomed, three-story historical mansion stands proudly, facing the tidal waterways. Palmettos, magnolias, and holly adorn its grounds, and antique furnishings decorate its interior.

Mrs. Sanders has lived at Frogmore Manor since the age of seven when her father, James Ross Macdonald, purchased it. When the white landowners fled before Union troops who captured the island in the 1861 battle of Port Royal, this plantation and other tracts of land were sold for taxes.

Laura Towne, one of Penn School's founding principals, bought Frogmore Manor during Reconstruction. After her death, the Macdonald family moved there.

"My mother (Clare I. Macdonald) was just eighteen when her mother died. She had just finished normal school in Philadelphia. She didn't know what was to become of her, what she was going to do. Laura Towne (a friend of Mrs. Sanders' grandmother) told her to come to St. Helena Island."

So Mrs. Sanders' mother journeyed south and taught first graders at Penn School, the first school built to educate blacks in the southern United States. "Many of the students were older than she was."

She met and soon thereafter married James Ross Macdonald, head of the Macdonald-Wilkins Company, which shipped the famous long-fibered Sea Island cotton to Savannah and Charleston. "Only about sixty white people and six thousand blacks lived on St. Helena at that time. Most of the white people worked for my father's firm."

Peacefulness and cooperativeness among the Island residents were as abundant as the land's tranquil beauty, Mrs. Sanders recalls. Through educational, financial and civic affiliations, the Macdonald family helped to mold the Islanders' history.

"Our family was always fond of the black familes on the Island. My father was the first person to introduce paying for the cotton (grown in home gardens) with hard money. Up to then, the people would barter for shoes, groceries and clothes. With their own money, they would buy what they needed. He felt they would be cheated elsewhere unless they were accustomed to dealing with currency."

15

Clare Macdonald left a legacy of St. Helena Island lore in *Recollections of Juliana*, a ten-page booklet about her house servant, published in 1924. Sales of the booklet were used to match community and foundational funds to establish the three-roomed Lee Rosenwald School (named for the Rosenwald Fund). Located at Coffin's Point Plantation, this school afforded an improvement to the common one-roomed schoolhouses.

The house servant Juliana was described as "tall, lean and straight, with high cheek bones like an Indian and the dark brown color of the Negro." According to Mrs. Macdonald, "She seemed to dominate the house."

Mrs. Macdonald wrote: "I had decided to retain Juliana because of long years of faithful service; but the air of benignant toleration with which she 'made her manners' led me to suspect that instead of magnanimously putting up with her, as I had intended, she was putting up with me.

"…I can see her now — standing half in and half out of the room — swinging the door to and fro, speaking the peculiar dialect which was almost a foreign tongue to me — regaling me with stories of 'Befo the war' to keep me 'from lonesome.' Her favorite tale was of Sherman's march through Winnsboro (South Carolina)."

Juliana's saga of freedom for St. Helena Island blacks, as recorded by Mrs. Macdonald, may very well be the only documented account of a native Islander:

"When the war bruk out all the white people be afraid to stay ober here on the islant, so dey done tuk we house serbants an' went to Beaufort. But, me fren! we want no better off dere. One night the Yankees' big guns boom all night an' shake ebery house in Beaufort like a ben a eart'quake. The nex' mornin' Miss Ann Elizabet tuk we all, an' we go away in a boat; but we ain't fine no safe place, so we hab to cum back an' take de train for Cha'ston. Jesus, me fren! what a whoopin' an' howlin' dere wuz dat day! All de ladies dey guine off an' take dere serbants wid dem, an' we ain't know where we guine, or if we ebber see home any mo'. We get to Cha'ston, but we ain't res' long dere,' an' we go on up country to Winnsboro. My Elizbet wuz a baby at dat time, an' I ben nussin' Miss Ann Elizabet's baby too. I tell you dat wuz a fine chile, dat Mannie! He reach out he arms to cum to me de minit he see me, an' Miss Ann Elizabet would say, 'Ain't you know yo' own modder dat bore you? Go away, Juliana, my chile loves you better'n me.'

"One day we hear dat Sherman's army wuz cumin' tru Winnsboro, en' all de white people dey mos' scared to deat'. Miss Ann Elizabet an' de res' dey go up to de top ob de house an' lock deyselves in; an' all we-uns t'row down ebbry t'ing an' run out to see de sojers. I ben walkin' out de gate wid Mannie in ma arms when Miss Ann Elizabet poke he head out de window an' call to me, 'Come back wid my chile, Juliana! Ain't you know dem Yankees is a-cumin' tru and I'll nebber see my chile again?'

"I say, 'Why, Miss Ann Elizabet, what dey guine do wid de chile?'

" ' Knock he brain out, for all I know!'

" 'Oh, no,' I say, 'dey ain't cruel like to dat; dey ain't hu't de chile.'

"Well, me fren! When I get up de street, what do I see? Sich a gang ob men, I ain't know dere wuz so many in de worl'; an' de drums go dumty, dum, dum, dum, an' sich a marching! All we-uns what cum out fer meet de army, we so scared, we ain't know what fer do. My knees trimble an' trimble an' ef I could-a run away I would, but my feet fair glued to de spot. When de men get up to me dey see Mannie, an' one ob de sojers tuk him outen me arms, an' I say, 'Jesus, me fren! Miss Ann Elizabet tell de truf. What I fer do?' But dem sojers nebber harm a hair ob he head. What you t'ink? Dey pass him along de line an' hug him up in dey bosom.

"Well, when I get back dat morning, Miss Ann Elizabet say, 'Juliana, go up to old Miss Patty's house; she told me to send for one of her tukrey an' we hab it fer dinner!' I too glad when I hear dat. Miss Patty hab too many tukrey an' chicken, an' we all ain't hab none cause we lef' dem all at home; but Miss Patty ain't nebber offer one ob her fowl to us befo', an' I tink to myself, 'De mean old ting! She only gib us one now 'cause she knows de Yankees will take dem anyhow.' Well, I go an' get de tukrey an' ben cumin' along wid it in ma han', when some sojers call out, 'Gal, where you get dat tukrey?' I tell dem at Miss Patty Robinson's, an' dey tu'n me roun' an' say, 'Show us de way!' an' dey take de tukrey from me and carry it deyselves.

"When we git to de house Ole Miss cum out an' say, 'I is a pore woman, I hasn't go anyt'ings in de house.' Well, dey go in de house an' ax for de bureau keys. Ole Miss say she loss dem. Den dey bruk open de drawers an' fine all de silver put away. Den dey say, 'Where de storeroom key?'

" ' I is a pore woman. I hasn't got anyt'ings dere.' Well, dey search roun' an' finally dey see where de eart' ben fresh dug up an' patted down in de ya'd an' dey dig dere an' fine de sto'room key. Dey open de do' an' fling out de t'ings. Dey tell Hannah an' me to help weselves, but we fraid Ole Miss. But dey say, 'Don't be afraid,' so I pitch in an' tuk all ma arms could hold. When dey done tuk eberytings dey ride off. Den Ole Miss say, 'Gal, pit down dose t'ings.'

"I say, 'De sojers give 'em to me.'

"She say, 'Pit 'em down. Dey ain't belongs to you. Dey are mine.' So I pit dem all down an' I go back widout tukrey nor nuttin' else.

17

"All de time de Yankees ben in Winnsboro, Miss Ann Elizabet' an' de res' watch we all night, 'cause dey fraid we run off. We-all hab to sleep along de porch an' dey take turns stayin' up to watch we. Some ob de sojers cum to de house, an' dey wuz as polite as could be, an' made fren's wid de chillun.

"...After de war we hear 'bout freedom, but we ain't know nuttin' fo' true. Miss Ann Elizabet' tell we niggers dat de Yankees hab set we free, but she say dey lick we harder den ebber. I say, 'None ain't guine lick Juliana. After you-all ain't lick me, what fo' de Yankees do um?' An' Miss Ann Elizabet' say:

" 'Mind, Juliana girl, you better mind.'

"Well, we all go on livin' peaceable 'til one day ma uncle an' brodder from St. Helena cum to take we'all home. Miss Ann say, 'So you guine to leave us, Juliana?'

"An' I say, 'Ef we ain't go now mebbe we nebber see home again.' So Miss Ann Elizabet' gave us bread an' meat an' t'ings to keep we from hongry on de way, an' de coach come to carry we-all to de depot."

Clare I. Macdonald, *Recollections of Juliana* (Columbia, South Carolina: The State Company, 1924), pp. 6, 9–13.

Mrs. Margaret M. Sanders died in January 1987.

18

A history of a people has been hushed, been stilled—

Netting and basket weaving were once popular folk arts on St. Helena Island.

People "toting" (carrying) articles on their heads was a common sight.

Islanders are gathered to witness a creek shore baptism.

Penn School, the first school in the South for blacks, was begun at this site, the Oaks Plantation House, in 1862. Penn School evolved into Penn Community Services, Inc., which Martin Luther King, Jr., visited frequently during the 1960s. Here he planned his 1963 March on Washington.

An instructor teaches below the shady oaks. Students walked miles along dirt roads or were ferried from distant islands to attain an education.

A male dormitory room at Penn School. Male and female students, many from nearby Hilton Head Island, boarded at least one year.

Rossa B. Cooley (right) and Grace Bigelow House served the Island following Penn School's founding principals, Laura Towne and Ellen Murray. The school changed the course of St. Helena's history by educating a newly freed people.

A group of midwives are assembled. Midwives were highly respected community members.

Through annual Baby Days, Islanders assured the health and longevity of their children. The child pictured displays a blue ribbon, signifying good health, as a midwife looks on proudly.

Dr. York W. Bailey served as the Island's first and only black doctor from 1906 until retirement in 1956. He was a graduate of Penn School and Hampton Institute in Virginia. The photograph is a copy of a pencil drawing by Winold Reiss, who composed many drawings of Islanders during the early 1900s. Several of Reiss's works are displayed in the Y. W. Bailey Cultural Center, Penn Community Services, Inc.

One-roomed schoolhouses were scattered about the Island. Until bridges and causeways to neighboring islands were constructed, teachers were ferried from St. Helena daily in rowboats.

The St. Helena Quartet, a renowned group of Penn School instructors, toured the United States to raise funds, performing Negro spirituals. Pictured are Aurelius "A. J." Brown, Benjamin "B. H." Washington, James "J. P." King, and Melvin T. Wildy.

Islanders, moving in a circle, are beginning a "Shout," a dance of praise. The Shout was accompanied by fervent spiritual singing and rhythmic hand clapping. The feet were moved energetically to the sides but never crossed, which would signify worldly dancing. [Photo used by permission of Mrs. Margaret M. Sanders.]

A horse-drawn mill was used for grinding sugar cane.

St. Helena and surrounding islands were renowned for their long-fibered "Sea Island" cotton.

An Island farmer threshes rice. Other principal crops were cotton, corn, sugar cane, potatoes, sweet potatoes.

Corn had to be ground on stone for grits and meal. The husks were fed to the hogs.

A community picnic is held at Ndulamo, where Penn School principals Rossa B. Cooley and Grace Bigelow House owned a retreat home. Housewarmings, another community event, were held after a house had been built. Community members would celebrate the owners' achievement by coming together, eating, praying, singing, and engaging in festivity.

Yet only few weep.
Only few sing the old songs

"De Ol' Sheep Done Kno' de Road"

De ol' sheep done kno' de road.
De ol' sheep done kno' de road.
De ol' sheep done kno' de road.
De young lam' mus' fin' de way.

Shout, my brotha, you are free!
 De young lam' mus' fin' de way.
Christ has brought your liberty!
 De young lam' mus' fin' de way.

De ol' sheep done kno' de road.
De ol' sheep done kno' de road.
De ol' sheep done kno' de road.
De young lam' mus' fin' de way.

Fight, my brotha, don't you run!
 De young lam' mus' fin' de way.
Don't go away 'til de battle is won!
 De young lam' mus' fin' de way.

De ol' sheep done kno' de road.
De ol' sheep done kno' de road.
De ol' sheep done kno' de road.
De young lam' mus' fin' de way.

"Good Lord, I Done Done"

Good Lord, I done done;
Good Lord, I done done;
Good Lord, I done done;
I done done what You tol' me to do.

You ast me to love, an' I done that, too.
You ast me to love, an' I done that, too.
You ast me to love, an' I done that, too.
I done done what You tol' me to do.

Good Lord, I done done;
Good Lord, I done done;
Good Lord, I done done;
I done done what You tol' me to do.

You ast me to pray, an' I done that, too.
You ast me to pray, an' I done that, too.
You ast me to pray, an' I done that, too.
I done done what You tol' me to do.

Good Lord, I done done;
Good Lord, I done done;
Good Lord, I done done;
I done done what You tol' me to do.

You ast me to sing, an' I done that, too.
You ast me to sing, an' I done that, too.
You ast me to sing, an' I done that, too.
I done done what You tol' me to do.

Good Lord, I done done;
Good Lord, I done done;
Good Lord, I done done;
I done done what You tol' me to do.

"I Don't Mind"

I don't mind; I don't mind.
I don't mind; I don't mind.
Long as my soul got a seat in the Kingdom,
I don't mind. I don't mind.

Mine, little brotha, how you walk on the cross —
Yo' feet might slip, an' yo' soul get los'!
Long as my soul got a seat in the Kingdom,
I don't mind. I don't mind.

I don't mind; I don't mind.
I don't mind; I don't mind.
Long as my soul got a seat in the Kingdom,
I don't mind. I don't mind.

Talk 'bout me much as you please —
Mo' you talk, I'm gonna ben' my knees!
Long as my soul got a seat in the Kingdom,
I don't mind. I don't mind.

I don't mind; I don't mind.
I don't mind; I don't mind.
Long as my soul got a seat in the Kingdom,
I don't mind. I don't mind.

"I'm a-Rollin'"

I'm a-rollin'.
I'm a-rollin'.
I'm a-rollin' through this unfriendly world.
I'm a-rollin'.
I'm a-rollin' through this unfriendly world.

Oh, Motha, won't you help me?
Oh, Motha, won't you help me to pray?
Oh, Motha, won't you help me?
Won't you help me in the service of the Lord?

I'm a-rollin'.
I'm a-rollin'.
I'm a-rollin' through this unfriendly world.
I'm a-rollin'.
I'm a-rollin' through this unfriendly world.

Oh, Fatha, won't you help me?
Oh, Fatha, won't you help me to pray?
Oh, Fatha, won't you help me?
Won't you help me in the service of the Lord?

I'm a-rollin'.
I'm a-rollin'.
I'm a-rollin' through this unfriendly world.
I'm a-rollin'.
I'm a-rollin' through this unfriendly world.

"Day Is Done"

Day is done.
Day is done.
Day is done.
I thank God day is done.

I work hard in the field all day.
    I thank God day is done.
But I'm never too tired to pray.
    I thank God day is done.

Day is done.
Day is done.
Day is done.
I thank God day is done.

E're I get to the mountain top —
    I thank God day is done.
I praise my God and never stop.
    I thank God day is done.

Day is done.
Day is done.
Day is done.
I thank God day is done.

Or recall precious moments.

Jennye Dudley remembers childhood years spent huddled with her mother and aunt around the fireplace. "We would sit by the fire at night, and my mother would just sing to me." Those moments, those songs have not been forgotten. The lyrics of those voices cannot be hushed.

Her memory conjures the lyrics of haunting slave songs, like "Nebber Me One to Hol' de Law."

"The song is about slaves worshipping God. They weren't allowed religious service. They were holding 'de law of God' when they stole away into the woods to worship — even if they had to do so alone, after others had died."

> Mudda gone.
> But me da hol' de law.
> Yes, Lawd, me da hol' de law.
> Mudda gone.
> But me da hol' de law.
> Yes, Lawd, me da hol' de law.
>
> Nebber me one
> T'hol' de law.
> Yes, Lawd, me da hol' de law.
> Nebber me one
> T'hol' de law.
> Yes, Lawd, me da hol' de law.

"They had interesting folk songs during my mother's time. There was always somebody to make up a song about."

She sings softly, with a twinkle in her eye, about the henpecked Casey Jones. The badgered husband left his wife Katie one night by boat, hoping to avoid capture on land before he had departed. His escape was triumphant, as the lyrics proclaim: "Casey Jones a-gone a long time — too so long for Katie."

Miss Dudley begins another lively tune. She pauses momentarily, tapping her right index finger to her forehead as if to nudge a forgotten lyric to memory. The song recounts the event of a jealous Island woman who fed her husband a cake laced with rat poison, killing him and "wounding" two others.

> Kate bought de flouah [flour] frum C'Pat [Cousin Pat].
> De powdah [powder] she use wuz de Rough on Rat [D-Con].
> For man, she bake de sweetes' bread —
> Wounded two and kill Green dead.
>
> Oh, de possum laugh.
> Oh, de possum laugh.

49

Gonna lib a long time.
Oh, de possum laugh.

"You see, the possum laughed because Green was a hunter, and he was a sure-shot. Green's death had assured his longevity. Those were some smart people to make up songs like that!"

The old folk songs, the old spirituals hold fond meaning for Miss Dudley.

"They have something to do with the appreciation of, and the trials of and deliverance from, slavery. When I sing them, I remember my aunt and mother singing them to me."

"I'm teaching on a Rock that will never give away."

Helping others to learn has meant much to Marjorie G. Seabrook. Her experiences began at South Pines School, a one-roomed building at Scott Plantation.

"The school building was not in the very best condition. One could stay inside and see the outside by looking through crevices of the walls and floors."

Yet her zeal remained undaunted. She had always yearned to teach and was following the profession of her father and three aunts.

"When I arrived at this particular school on the very first morning, I was amazed to find so many children. There were as many as sixty or more pupils waiting eagerly to be taught."

She was teacher and principal as well. In order to be near the school, she lived with families in the neighborhood. Even with this arrangement, she walked about two miles each day throughout the six-month school year.

For her second teaching assignment, a student ferried her daily to nearby Warsaw Island.

"Sometimes the ferryman would yell, 'You got high win' an' 'gin tide.' That meant the wind was 'a-gin,' or against, us — and the tide was against us. Sometimes I encountered high tide, and sometimes I encountered low tide. When the tide was high, it was favorable for me. This meant that the boat could go nearer to dry land. But when it was low, it was unfavorable. For then I had to walk in a great deal of mud before reaching high land."

To keep warm on cold mornings, Mrs. Seabrook bundled herself in extra clothing and wore a pair of men's boots to keep her feet dry. Following the hour-long transport, she walked about a mile and a half to the schoolhouse.

"The building was cold. Fire was made in a trash burner, using wood that pupils had gathered the previous day.

"Even though I did not like traveling across the water, I enjoyed teaching on Warsaw Island. I visited many of the homes. This gave me a better insight into some of the problems that existed. Home visits played a tremendous role in helping to bridge the gaps between the homes and school."

During inclement weather, she remained on Warsaw Island with families of the forty first- through sixth-graders. "These were very hospitable people. They took me in at no cost at all!"

Mrs. Seabrook's monthly salary from 1929–1935 was about $35.

"Of course, this amount could buy a great deal in those days! During my early years, teachers had to buy plenty of materials used. A lot of my own money would be spent in making things look right for the children and for buying pencils and crayons."

51

Throughout her 41-year teaching career, Mrs. Seabrook lived up to the motto of her five-member Penn School graduating class: "Enter to learn; go out to serve."

"I'm glad that I was able to help somebody to learn to write and read. Whenever I come in contact with the children whose lives I helped to mold, I feel a sense of proudness."

"Get right, children; get right. Oh, yes, Lord."

Preparations culminated the night before, as St. Helena Islanders readied for Farmers' Fair.

Farmers scrutinized their produce — corn, sugar cane, pumpkins, rice, peanuts and sweet potatoes — selecting the most appealing. In the morning, they would load their healthiest pigs, horses and cows.

Housewives added finishing touches to quilts, dresses and other homespun items. Their jarred fruits would spice the atmosphere at the following day's fair, and their jarred vegetables would tantalize onlookers' eyes. Everyone was hopeful for a first prize.

A good time was assured.

"By morning, the (Penn School) grounds would be covered," muses Kathleen G. Daise. "It was a big affair. Everyone was welcomed to bring whatever he had — things made or raised during the year."

The festivities were seasoned with anticipation, not only for prize winning, but for the traditional Farmers' Fair barbecue, as well.

"It was started the night before . . . ." Mr. Josie Holmes, under the supervision of the school farm superintendent, labored long over a big iron pot. With a new pitchfork, he stirred in the beef of freshly slaughtered cows, along with rice, potatoes and appetizing seasonings. "People would be lined up from way back! That was some good barbecue!"

The Island students began celebrating Farmers' Fair (with recitations, skits, plays and songs) a day earlier than the adults. The annual two-day observance molded within the youths a sense of community spirit, cooperation and tradition.

Children from outlying one- to three-roomed county schools would journey to Penn School to integrate their performances with the Pennites'. Mrs. Daise recalls a Farmers' Fair tune presented by students from the Eddings Point Plantation School.

My hand, my hand, my hand,
My hand, my hand, my hand —
You must learn to wash and iron
And keep your dishes clean!

"I liked the getting together and communicating with people from all over the Island, and seeing all the different things people had raised. It was a day everyone looked forward to!"

Baby Day, another annual celebration, attested to the Islanders' zest for independence.

"Mothers were always proud of their babies and looked forward to the next Baby Day," continues Mrs. Daise. "That was the day mothers took their babies to the Penn School campus to be weighed and measured. All the midwives were there. All the healthy babies received blue ribbons; others, honorable mention.

"It taught mothers to try to keep their babies (infant to four years old) healthy. There were always a number of blue-ribbon babies because the mothers would try to live up to what the midwives were teaching them: how to care for the baby, how to bathe him, and what kind of food to give him.

"All of mine were blue-ribbon babies!" Mrs. Daise boasts about four of her nine children born before the event was terminated. School buses, called 'chariots,' transported mothers to the school grounds. "I didn't go one year. The chariot came by with mothers on it . . ."

Mrs. Daise, however, gave birth to her fifth child on that May morning.

"Baby Day ensured that Island mothers would bring healthy babies into the world," she adds. "It was an all-day affair!"

Midwives were respected and celebrated. Maggie "Miss Mary" Smalls is a witness.

"When patients saw a midwife coming, they thought they saw heaven! They thought the midwife could ease their burdens for them."

She began midwifery in 1941, at age forty-five. During her five-year practice, she delivered more than two thousand St. Helena Island babies.

"Sarah Gibbes Thompson — she trained me. She said she was getting old and couldn't get around like she used to. She asked me if I would be interested."

Cleanliness and patience, a midwife's most important qualities, were learned following a two-week workshop for certification at Benedict College, Columbia, South Carolina. "Cleanliness is next to godliness. And you have to have patience in working with people — and a good mind to work. Lots of people figured everything would happen in a rush. But you had to wait.

"Sometimes I would get a call in the middle of the night, but the patient wasn't ready. Some wanted me to stay right there. They didn't want me to leave them. But I had to leave them."

Her husband and thirteen-member family, including two adopted children, needed caring for when a birth wasn't imminent. When patients insisted she stay with them even though the situation wasn't an emergency, she remedied them with advice.

"I would just politely give them consolation. I told them not to worry. When their time came, they would know. I'd crack a lot of jokes. They liked to hear us crack jokes because they would laugh. They figured that would ease their burden.

"Sometimes I had five patients in a week. I could get in more patients than the rest because they had to walk." Mrs. Smalls, however, traveled in her black 1942 Ford.

"I worked all over this Island — in Wallace, Scott, Land's End, Cuffie, Coffin's Point, Fripp Point, Cedar Grove, Capers and Warsaw." A midwife's fee when Smalls began her practice was $6 for girls and $7 for boys. She never questioned the difference in costs.

"Before the baby came, you had to visit them [expectant mothers] three times so they could get everything prepared. After birth, you had to visit them each day until they got up. They had to lie down on their backs for nine days (after delivering a baby). And, at that time, when you got up, you were too weak to walk. Nowadays, at the hospital, they make you get up the same day. Some of them had the strength back then, too. But the old people believed they had to stay in bed. They couldn't see no sunlight."

Many homes were void of baby-care items. In some, quilts folded in a dresser drawer served as makeshift cribs; pieces of burlap wrapped around a teaspoonful of sugar, as pacifiers. "I helped them out as much as I could."

Her work enriched her — even though some patients have never paid.

"Some of the babies I delivered have died and gone to heaven, and the parents haven't paid me yet. Some patients were like the frog when the snake caught him. . . ."

She laughs an arid cackle, yet her eyes are filled with humor. Amusement is the offspring of her tale:

". . . The frog say, 'Turn me loose!' Then when the snake had turned him loose, he forgot. That's how they did me."

Mrs. Maggie Smalls died in February 1987.

"You ast me to sing, an' I done that, too!"

"They used to beg for us!"

Aurelius "A. J." Brown reminisced about his fifteen years as a member of the famed St. Helena Quartet. Its repertoire of Negro spirituals was heard throughout the United States as the group traveled to raise money for Penn School.

Brown and his friends thrilled audiences with "Go Down, Moses," "He Ain't Comin' Here to Die No More," "When the Rocks and the Mountains Shall All Flee Away," and "Lead Me to the Rock That Is Higher Than I."

"We had a good quartet!" Its fame mounted higher and higher. Whenever a certain gentleman heard the group perform, he donated $50 or $100.

"We went to Boston, Maine and Philadelphia. The thrill of my life was when we sang at the British Embassy in Washington, D.C. It was a great big assembly hall, with dignitaries and so many people. That place was the most beautiful I've ever seen. From that performance, we must have raised more than $20,000."

Singing was an important part of Brown's life even while he was a Penn School student. Each class had a quartet that competed at the end of the school year. After Brown became the Penn School instructor of leather crafts, shoe repair and harness making, his love for singing continued. A second tenor, he eventually replaced an original Quartet member and, with the group, entertained friends of Penn School whenever they visited the campus. The Quartet also performed during monthly Community Sings, church functions and other community celebrations.

Brown and other Island songsters cheered the community during a major Christmas event, the Mystery Play. Brown portrayed a shepherd in this production that heralded the Christmas story. Held in the school gymnasium every two years from 1916 through 1962, the play highlighted spirituals and traditional Old English carols sung with a Sea Island flavor. Brown soloed, "Rise Up, Shepherds, and Follow," "The Shepherds' Song," and "Go Tell It on the Mountains."

The caroling continued out-of-doors, also.

"Every Christmas, we would serenade the people of the Island with Christmas carols. They'd have cake or wine on the tables waiting for us. We'd start out about twelve midnight Christmas morning and sing until day clean (dawn)!"

In the calm and stillness of early morning, Islanders would be awakened by melodies of "Silent Night," "Lo, What a Branch of Beauty," and other favorites.

"Folks looked forward to our coming. We were called 'angels.'"

Brown died June 11, 1981.

Time, progress and shortsightedness
are silencing a heritage!

From generation to generation, Islanders could pass down the pride inherent to those who are land-owners and not slaves.

Trades vital to daily sustenance were taught during the early 1900s: basketry, carpentry, cobbling, harness making, wheelwrighting, machine repair and blacksmithing.

Having access to a black-operated cooperative society, credit union, community class, homemaker's club and other public service organizations helped instill a sense of worth and pride in the Islanders.

An unhurried lifestyle and a deep abiding faith in God characterized the Islanders' daily lives.
These sentiments are expressed in the lyrics of their spirituals.

The palmetto branch was employed to discern whether an individual had spoken untruthfully about theft. With two palmetto leaves placed on either side of the accused's neck, the person performing the ritual would command the fronds to "Tie, palmetto, tie" if a lie had been told. According to lore, the green blades would entwine around a liar's neck, beginning to choke him.

Whenever a family member died, survivors would mourn the death for a year by dressing only in black when appearing in public. Some dressed in black even in their homes. If a deacon died, a black bow was affixed somewhere in the church for one year. A deceased preacher's chair in the church was draped in black cloth. No one could be seated in it for a year.

The elderly were treated customarily with respect. They were believed to have the power to "put mouth," a curse of unfavorable circumstances, on the disrespectful individual.

According to Rev. Isaiah Middleton, a Baptist minister who pastored on the Island from 1948 to 1982, the expression "let mornin' star greet you on yo' prayin' groun'" began during slavery. Because they weren't allowed to worship openly, slaves sneaked to their "prayin' grounds" in the woods late at night. The morning star was their timepiece. When it started twinkling, slaves knew morning would soon follow. They then returned home before they were missed, escaping being whipped.

Baptism was the culmination of an Island custom known as "seekin' religion in the wilderness." The baptismal candidates are dressed in white.

Religion and spirituality were highly esteemed, although peculiarities such as "turning the Bible" were common to the area. To determine if someone had lied about an action, a giant key was placed within a Bible (with the pages facing downward) at a certain text of the gospel of St. Matthew. The person performing the ritual would recite: "By St. Peter, by St. Paul, by the grace of the good Lord who made us all, if (name of suspect followed by the allegation), I pray, Bible, you will turn and fall." Reportedly, the Bible would flip over the key and fall if the accusation was true.

A fireplace at night was a probable site for reliving local ghost tales. One tale was of "the hag," which supposedly sat on people's faces at night as they slept, disorienting and terrorizing them.

Children were admonished to be respectful and mannerly to adults. Sass and back talk were not tolerated. The students pictured march to class.

Precious memories, though,
Are like the lyrics of old slave songs.

"I'm Standing on a Solid Rock"

I'm standing on a Solid Rock.
I'm standing on a Solid Rock.
I'm standing on a Rock that will never give away.
I'm standing on a Solid Rock.

Jesus is the Solid Rock.
Jesus is the Solid Rock.
Jesus is the Rock that will never give away.
Jesus is the Solid Rock.

I'm praying on a Solid Rock.
I'm praying on a Solid Rock.
I'm praying on a Rock that will never give away.
I'm praying on a Solid Rock.

I'm teaching on a Solid Rock.
I'm teaching on a Solid Rock.
I'm teaching on a Rock that will never give away.
I'm teaching on a Solid Rock.

I'm standing on a Solid Rock.
I'm standing on a Solid Rock.
I'm standing on a Rock that will never give away.
I'm standing on a Solid Rock.

Testimonies of strength in the Almighty

. . . gratitude for deliverance

"How I Got Ovah"

How I got ovah.
How I got ovah.
I look back an' wondah how I got ovah.

Went down to the valley one day to pray.
   I look back an' wondah how I got ovah.
My soul got happy an' I stayed all day!
   I look back an' wondah how I got ovah.

I prayed an' got ovah.
I prayed an' got ovah.
I look back an' wondah how I got ovah.

I never been t'Heaven but I been tol' —
   I look back an' wondah how I got ovah.
The streets up there are pave' with gold.
   I look back an' wondah how I got ovah.

I sang an' got ovah.
I sang an' got ovah.
I look back an' wondah how I got ovah.

If you get there befo'e I do —
   I look back and wondah how I got ovah.
Tell all my friends I'm comin', too!
   I look back an' wondah how I got ovah.

My God brought me ovah!
My God brought me ovah!
I look back an' wondah how I got ovah!

"Prayer Will Bring You Out All Right"

Prayer will bring you out all right!
Prayer will bring you out all right!
You just take your feet out of the miry clay —
Prayer will bring you out all right!

Brought my father out all right!
Brought my father out all right!
You just take your feet out of the miry clay —
Prayer will bring you out all right!

Brought my mother out all right!
Brought my mother out all right!
You just take your feet out of the miry clay —
Prayer will bring you out all right!

Prayer brought me out all right!
Prayer brought me out all right!
You just take your feet out of the miry clay —
Prayer will bring you out all right!

Prayer will bring you out all right!
Prayer will bring you out all right!
You just take your feet out of the miry clay —
Prayer will bring you out all right!

. . . endurance for life's battles

. . . hope during moments of discouragement

"Dere's a Bright Side Somewhere"

Dere's a bright side somewhere.
Dere's a bright side somewhere.
I'm gonna keep on 'til I find it.
Dere's a bright side somewhere.

Dere is mo' love somewhere.
Dere is mo' love somewhere.
I'm gonna keep on 'til I find it.
Dere is mo' love somewhere.

Dere is mo' joy somewhere.
Dere is mo' joy somewhere.
I'm gonna keep on 'til I find it.
Dere is mo' joy somewhere.

Dere is mo' peace somewhere.
Dere is mo' peace somewhere.
I'm gonna keep on 'til I find it.
Dere is mo' peace somewhere.

Dere's a bright side somewhere.
Dere's a bright side somewhere.
I'm gonna keep on 'til I find it.
Dere's a bright side somewhere.

"Feel Like Journey On"

Well, I come this far, fin' no fault, feel like journey on.
Come this far, fin' no fault, feel like journey on.

If religion wuz a thing that money could buy —
  Feel like journey on.
The rich would live an' the po' would die!
  Feel like journey on.

Well, I come this far, fin' no fault, feel like journey on.
Come this far, fin' no fault, feel like journey on.

The Jerden Rivah is chilly an' col' —
  Feel like journey on.
It chills my body but not my soul.
  Feel like journey on.

Well, I come this far, fin' no fault, feel like journey on.
Come this far, fin' no fault, feel like journey on.

Upon the mountain, my God spoke —
  Feel like journey on.
Out of His mouth came fire an' smoke!
  Feel like journey on.

Well, I come this far, fin' no fault, feel like journey on.
Come this far, fin' no fault, feel like journey on.

. . . confidence in facing every tomorrow.

They should not be
Stored up
In the minds of
A few.

Six-year-old Ruben Fripp learned shrimp netting from his father. Today the craft, brought to the Island from the West African coast, still throbs within his hands.

A short, gray-bearded man, Fripp walks the highway throughout the day, dressed in a dark or gray suit and white shirt. He carries a black satchel, a black radio and nets to be completed. A pipe juts from his back pocket. At stop signs, he stops, attaches his nets and begins working.

In and out, his hands weave. Up and down. He loops bonded nylon around a finger on his left hand. And swings the threader in his right hand throughout the air.

"Just like a typewriter," he explains. "You gotta learn to use all your fingers [as you would] on the keys.

"My daddy taught me this in 1930 and '31. He learned netting from an old woman on Eustis Plantation. This is just a hobby. I don't make any [vast amount of] money from it. I know the fellas [his customers]. They always give me a ride on the road. I don't charge them much. I guarantee ya they'll work right. Or I'll fix them free of charge."

Net making, like quilting and basket weaving, is a dying folk art on St. Helena Island.

A retired bricklayer and construction worker, Fripp boasts: "I can net in the dark without light!" The nylon thread cuts him frequently, but Fripp perseveres. He rubs the area with Vaseline and salt to harden the skin. "The harder your hand gets, the more you can net. I can net all day!"

Fripp's portable radio provides company during solitary moments of work. But usually passersby stop to talk or merely admire. Although he hardly refuses to chat, the rhythm of his hands never ceases.

The rhythm, the motion, the concentration of eyes and hands are spectacular. For Fripp loves his labor. His zeal is a lesson to many.

Before her death in 1982, another memorable folk artist, Jane Chisholm, expressed her love for painting and embellishing seashells and driftwood. Although not an Island native, she touched the lives of many through her artistry.

Her work, she confided, was her prayer.

Her 23-year-old son Ralph telephoned her from New York City one Saturday night. "He was coming home to stay." Just out of the U.S. Army, Ralph was returning to St. Helena Island to open a business. "He had called home to tell me what he wanted me to fix him for breakfast."

When the telephone rang the following morning, Mrs. Chisholm was mounting a large bird. A creation of folk art, the completed project is made of painted oyster shells and real bird feathers. But Mrs. Chisholm didn't complete the bird

83

that Sunday morning. The telephone message was from the New York City airport. Ralph had died of a heart attack while awaiting his flight.

"I was so mixed up! It was like I didn't have any sense!"

The memory of her first son's death was still throbbing in her thoughts; Kenneth, eighteen, had died the very day he was graduated from the Manual Training School in New Jersey.

"I cried all through the graduation service. All he got was honors."

Her tears of joy, however, became tears of grief after she and her husband Lawrence returned home. Kenneth had stayed behind to perform with the Boys' Quartet. He was to have joined his parents in Ridgewood, New Jersey the following day, and he rode on the running board of their car until they got past the school gate.

"That was the last I saw of him!"

The car the quartet members were in went down an embankment. Kenneth was the only one to die.

"That was something I thought I would never forget! I wasn't going to pray anymore!" Her faith ebbed, but her labor consoled her.

"You can't do nothing without God!" asserted the native of Nassau, Bahamas. Her labor became her prayer. Quilting, weaving, painting, decorating seashells and driftwood busied her hands and soothed her thoughts.

"God gave me more faith each time I woke up from that sorrow and frustration. He made me stronger. It made me a real person, one who could stand and take the hardships.

"I [would] wake up at night and just work on these things. I think that if you have a feeling to do something — and it's something that's good, then you should do it. That's what God wants you to do."

84

Charles "Dan" Watson distinctly remembers his mother's words.
"My mother would tell me to be sure and be out there (in the woods) at four in the morning because that was the time the Lord would be coming by. If I was in the house, she would wake me up and send me out. I had to go. I had to do what the folks said."

Watson, at twenty-two, was joining Scottville Baptist Church. As dictated by Sea Island tradition, his mother was encouraging him to go "seeking." True religion had to be found by "going into the wilderness."

Fervent prayer was essential to "seeking." Seekers were supposed to see visions in dreams. In turn, their dreams would be interpreted by an older person designated or chosen as their spiritual teacher.

"I knew from the very beginning that I wanted Louisa Aiken to be my spiritual teacher. She was a good woman. I would go to her every evening, and she would interpret my dreams. I was a long time seeking. I guess I was about two months."

Each seeker wore a white cloth tied around his forehead and had to dream of something white before his spiritual teacher pronounced that he had "come through." The new convert then met at the prayer house (one on each plantation) to receive oral catechism from the prayer leader until the appropriate responses had been memorized.

"What are you going to do with your former friends?" the leader would ask. "Are you going to keep them?"

The response, which had to include addressing the the leader as "Sir," was: "Yessir, I'm going to keep them and pray that the Lord will change them as He changed po' me."

Creek shore baptisms were performed only during the morning ebb tide, according to belief that the receding waters would wash away the believer's sins into the ocean's depths.

"I can understand now that they [church leaders and older Island residents] didn't understand about the 'wilderness,'" Watson adds. "All the saying means is that when you're not in the ark of safety, when you don't believe in God — you are in the 'wilderness.'"

With a resounding tenor voice, Watson sings "My Soul Is a Witness," his favorite spiritual. The verses expound the exploits of biblical characters Methuselah, Samson and Daniel:

> You read in the Bible, an' you understan'
> Methuselah wuz the oldes' man.
> He live nine hundred an' sixty-nine
> An' died an' went to heav'n in due-season time.

85

Methuselah wuz a witness for my Lord!
Methuselah wuz a witness for my Lord!

You read in the Bible, an' you understan'
Samson wuz the stronges' man.
Samson went out at one time
An' slew one t'ousan' of the Philistine.
Delilah fool Samson, this you kno',
For the holy Bible tell us so.
She shave off his head jus' as clean as yo' han',
An' his stren't became the same as any nat'ral man.
Samson wuz a witness for my Lord!
Samson wuz a witness for my Lord!

Now Daniel wuz a Hebrew chile.
He went an' he prayed to his God awhile.
The king at once for Daniel did sen',
An' he put him right down in the lion's den.
God sent His angel, the lion to keep.
An' Daniel lay down an' went to sleep.
Daniel wuz a witness for my Lord!
Daniel wuz a witness for my Lord!

Who will be a witness for my Lord?
Who will be a witness for my Lord?
My soul is a witness for my Lord!
My soul is a witness for my Lord!

"I know the Lord has laid His hands on me!"

Rev. Isaiah H. Middleton was called to be a preacher: his mother foresaw it in a vision six days before he was born.

The eighth of nine children born to Charlie and Maria Middleton, he was named for the Prophet Isaiah. As he narrates, his voice peaks from a whisper to a high shriek. He closes one eye and stares fixedly to emphasize a point while recalling the significance his mother attached to his naming.

Middleton's Granny, or midwife, thought the baby Isaiah would not live. So his mother gave him the middle name "Handy."

"If he lives, he'll come in handy," she had prophesied. "So call him 'Handy'!"

Thunderous and contagious laughter complete the storytelling. And Middleton stretches his eyes in amusement. True to his mother's foretelling, Middleton pursued the ministry. He pastored the Adams Street Baptist Church, Land's End Plantation, for 34 years beginning in 1948.

For someone to receive a calling through prophetic visions or dreams, according to widespread belief, testifies to his closeness with God. Emanuel "Mannie" Alston, an Island deacon well known for perpetuating the "old-time religion" through trumpeting and thunderous praying and sing-til-the-power-of-the-Lord-comes-down hymn leading, recounts his calling to church service.

A knock on his door one night awoke the 30-year-old Alston. Upon opening it, he met two strangers, a man and a woman dressed in plain clothing. They came into his front room.

"He was not a white man. They were colored."

The gentleman told him: "I want you to be an officer in the work of the Lord. If you don't, I'm going to whip you!"

Alston dropped his head and asked the man to repeat his words. With a finger pointed directly at Alston's face, the mysterious caller responded: "I want you to be an officer in the work of the Lord. If you don't, I'm going to whip you!"

"If you want me to do it, master, I'll do it!" Alston answered.

The gentleman then tucked a book under his arm, and the pair walked away.

"I never saw him before. And I [have] never seen him since!"

A few Sundays following the incident, Alston was asked to become a deacon at Ebenezer Baptist Church. He readily accepted.

The Baptist Church wielded immense influence among the Islanders throughout the early 1900s. Deacons, as well as preachers, oversaw civil disputes and spiritual matters. Police enforcement was sought only in extreme instances.

A concern first was heard by the deacons in the prayer houses on each plantation. If it could not be resolved here, it was taken before the church congregation. Should the member decide not to abide by the congregation's ruling, he would be placed "on the back seat." In other words, he could attend church services, but he was silenced from participating in church affairs until he petitioned the church for forgiveness. Subsequently, all of his rights and privileges as a church member were restored.

"I nevah seen such a man befo'e."

Until one of St. Helena's native sons returned to doctor his people, home remedies were used faithfully.

Some Islanders utilized nature's medications. To combat the common cold, for instance, lifeverlasting, whorehound and mullein (wild herbs) were brewed and drunk. Mint, a plant that flourished in low, damp areas (usually around hand-pumps) also was brewed as tea and given for indigestion and heartburn. Children with intestinal worms chewed Jerusalem, a weed with pointed leaves resembling a Christmas tree.

Oil bush, a green plant with wide leaves, or the leaves of the lily bush were gathered for sufferers of high fever. The individual would be wrapped with the leaves around his upper body and thighs and covered in bed until the fever had been sweated out.

Other remedies, though, were based on folk beliefs and superstitions. Headaches were treated by tying cord tightly around one's head. Another cure for cold was to eat a mixture of one teaspoon of sugar and a few drops of kerosene. A compound of mashed Octagon soap and sugar would be packed into a cut or gash. In other instances, the blossom of an okra plant would be tied to the affected area.

Cured pork skin was needed for curing the mumps. It would be lain flat on a strip of cloth. With the salted skin resting against the person's throat, the cloth would be tied atop the head and worn until the swelling had subsided.

Root, or hoodoo, beliefs accounted for other remedies. For example, whenever someone developed a persistent itch on the bottom of his foot, he was told to scratch his foot on a tombstone or with a stick from a graveyard.

Dr. York W. Bailey became the Island's only resident doctor in 1906, amidst such widespread superstitious beliefs. A graduate of Penn School, he furthered his studies at Hampton Institute in Virginia and Howard University in Washington, D.C. His fifty years of service as the Island's first black doctor provided proper medical care to his community. The Island residents had no money to pay him during his early years of practice, so he was compensated with corn, peas, chickens, ducks or turkeys, which he sold in Beaufort.

89

"If you get there befo'e I do, tell all my friends I'm comin', too!"

Agnes C. Sherman relates the following account of Labor Day celebrations on St. Helena Island:

"In the early 1900s, the Labor Day Celebration on the 'Green' was a festive affair!

"The day climaxed the end of summer vacation. So native St. Helena Islanders relocated throughout the United States returned home for their last homecoming day of the year. Boat excursions from Savannah, Georgia, arrived early in the morning, docking at the 'yard,' a harbor on Fuller Plantation.

"Visitors joined the crowd of local Islanders for a gala celebration at the picnic ground, known as the 'Bay' or the 'Green.' Because there were no cars on the Island during that period, men, women and children walked the miles of shelled and boggy sand roads to the picnic ground. The more fortunate traveled in oxen carts, horse and buggies or 'gigs,' one-seat vehicles that carried up to four people sitting in each other's laps.

"The event was sponsored by the Young Men's Social Club, an organization of men from various plantations about the Island. Tables and concession stands set up by individuals from Lady's Island and St. Helena Island featured delicacies such as red rice, hoppin' John (brown field peas cooked with rice), fish, crabs, shrimp, fried chicken and ham.

"Dessert dishes included homemade doughnuts, pies, cakes, candy and ice cream made in hand-operated churns. Refreshing pink lemonade would complete the menu. Doughnuts sold for one cent; and a small dip of ice cream, for two cents.

"The sack race, potato race and horse shoe toss were favored activities. But the most exciting contest of the day unfolded as boys took turns climbing a greasy pole to get a dollar bill at the top. Their attempts to scale the slick pole were humorous. But one persevering youth eventually would make it to the top and claim the money as his prize!

"Beaufort County's first black policemen patrolled during the affair. These men, selected by the Beaufort Police Department, were responsible for keeping order on the picnic ground. Chief of Police Clarence L. Polite, better known as 'Junk Polite,' is remembered for his ability to handle disorderly participants. Rowdy picnic-goers were tried and fined according to the offense. The upper story of the Knights of Wiseman Hall (still standing adjacent the 'Green') was used as the jailhouse.

"The Cedar Grove and Warsaw Island Bands and the Allen Brass Band of Beaufort enlivened the participants with music, causing heads to sway and fingers to snap. Popular dance steps were the 'one-step, two-step,' 'waltz,' 'ball-a-jack' and the 'buck,' a specialty of the men.

"Late in the afternoon, the celebration would begin to end. The excursion boat whistle would sound, beckoning out-of-towners to board for the return trip to Savannah. And the Island residents would begin their long trek back home, walking the shelled and boggy sand roads."

90

"Don't you be like the foolish virgins when the Bridegroom come."

St Helena Island history is incomplete without acknowledgment of Penn School. Graduates treasure fond memories of activities that stressed the importance of being standard bearers in their community and of being prepared for any opportunity. A more comprehensive study is left to historians devoted to its story.

The historic institution, the first school for blacks in the South, was founded in 1862 by northern missionaries for the educating of freed slaves. Laura M. Towne of Philadelphia and Ellen Murray of London, England, began classes in a room of the Oaks Plantation House with a meager enrollment of nine women. This humble undertaking had been launched as part of the Port Royal Experiment, designed to ease the transition from slavery to freedom. Teachers were sent by northern missionary associations. Charlotte Forten, a black teacher from Philadelphia, soon joined Miss Towne, along with Grace Bigelow House and Rossa B. Cooley, Murray's successor.

Enrollment flourished, and classes soon were moved to the Brick Baptist Church (built in 1855). The school, named for Quaker leader William Penn, was laid out amidst stately oaks draped with Spanish moss, on property adjoining the church grounds.

Its program encompassed industrial and agricultural education, which equipped the Islanders to become self-proficient. Teacher training, too, was provided. The trades taught included carpentry, blacksmithing, wheelwrighting, cobbling and harness making, basketry, machine repair, farming, sewing, laundering, cooking, housekeeping, dairying and poultry raising.

Through its numerous community activities and services, the school enabled many to realize the freedom expressed in the opening stanza of the ''St. Helena Hymn'' (written by poet John Greenleaf Whittier):

Oh, none in all the world before
    Were ever glad as we.
We're free on Carolina's shore.
    We're all at home and free!

Penn School, thus, became known as ''A Light to the Islands.'' To prepare the newly freed slaves for productive lives, the school embraced programs in land ownership, industry, temperance and literacy. Community organizations included the Midwives' Class, to engender better health and child care; Community Class, to host health discussions and make quilts for the needy; Home Makers' Club, to foster beautification of homes and yards, canning, handicraft, health and home sanitation; and the Folklore Society, to preserve the dialect, folk games and songs.

Also, there were the Cooperative Society, an organization allowing the farmers to market together and purchase fertilizer in large quantities; Credit Union; Corn Club, for boys; Garden Club, for girls; and other religious, youth and public service organizations.

91

Self-determination, self-pride and pride in and responsibility toward one's community were stressed. Principal Rossa B. Cooley, in the school's 75-year anniversary handbook, urged all: "Go forth, press forward, and lead St. Helena and other Sea Islands to Better Days."

They should linger—
From generation to generation—

"An' the world can't do me no ha'm!"

With mere imagination and ingenuity, Sea Island youths would amuse
themselves untiringly.

Little girls had few manufactured dolls (some, donated by Northerners,
were given as Christmas presents to students). Yet corn-shuck dolls were plentiful.
After the green corn husks had been peeled, the cob was adorned with scraps
of material for clothing. The tannish shuck remained as "hair" to be plaited,
combed and pampered.

Making mud pies was another favored pastime. Under shady trees, girls would
"play house," preparing their dirt delicacies in discarded cans and can lids and
serving their guests on oyster shell plates.

Young boys nailed the tops of cans to each end of a stick or pole. The newly
"wheeled" toy was then pushed happily about the yard. Others practiced batting
and pitching with sticks, stones and pine cones, dreaming of the day they would join
older males on plantation baseball teams that enlivened sultry summer afternoons.

Some children tied strings around June bugs (known as fig-eaters), and, holding
the string in one hand, listened to the destructive insects' wings drone as they
spiraled about. Another pastime was catching fireflies and placing them in jars,
being careful to punch holes in the tops for ventilation. At night, watching the
insects illuminate at close range was exciting.

During school recess, ring games were played with zest. With hands interlocked
and swinging up and down vigorously, they sang: "Sally over the water; Sally
over the sea. Sally caught a big fish, but Sally can't catch me!" The name of the
child whose arms became disengaged was substituted in the succeeding verse.

"Go in and out the window" was another favorite. One child weaved in and
out of the ring as the children chanted:

Go in and out the window.
Go in and out the window.
Go in and out the window
As we have done before.

During the second verse, "Go forth and chose your lover," the child in center
ring stood in front of his/her "lover." The following verses were "I measure my
love to show you," "Come follow me to London," and "Now choke him/her
'til he/she hollers!"

An oft-repeated rhyme was:

I pawn(ed) my watch.
I pawn(ed) my chain.
I pawn(ed) my last ten dollar bill.

95

An' if I had ten dollars mo'e.
I'd make my home in Baltimo'e!
Oh, gee, oh-ho!
I'm gonna shake my sugar down!

The "sugar" would be "shaken down" as youths twisted and cavorted their bottoms with glee. The cadence of Sea Island rhymes afforded hand-clappin' and foot-stompin' fun for girls playing Pat-a-Cake or jumping rope.

Boys' games included tossing horse shoes, playing bingo, football or baseball, fishing, shooting marbles, or wrestling. For music making, girls would blow hair combs draped with tissue paper or waxed paper; boys would play homemade whistles whittled from hollow cane.

Games also were played at social outings for older youths. These events were school or church sponsored and chaperoned by parents. In addition to musical chairs, the Grand March was a customary activity. The Grand March was undertaken with boys and girls pairing off, interlocking arms and marching about the room until the music had ended. Few activities allowed such intimate physical contact between the sexes.

The Cake Walk was a game played for a prize: a cake, homemade and scrumptious and on display. As music was played, participants walked about the floor, which had numbers scattered on it. When the music ended, everyone scrambled to stand on a number — which, hopefully, matched the number designated for the cake.

"Early one mornin', Death come creepin' in m'room!"

Mrs. Martha Jenkins of Coffin's Point Plantation tells an eerie tale:
"My cousin an' some other boys went huntin' one day. An' they hunt all through the graveyard. An' while they was in there, he pick up this clock off of one of the graves an' brought it home an' clean it up. After cleanin' it, it start to run. So he put it on his dresser in his room.

"That night after he went to bed, ev'rytime he doze off, that thing tell him: 'Bring my clock back!'

"That went on all night. An' early the nex' mornin', he got his brother with him, an' he took that clock back! An' that person did not bother him anymore!"

The Sea Islands are noted as a haven of lingering spirits. Tales of haints and hags abound, as well as belief in root doctors, hoodoo, or black magic.

A dying custom, most probably of African origin, called for placing a dead person's personal effects — pipes, pots, and pans, jewelry, clocks — upon his grave. Accordingly, a person's "spirit," when freed from the grave, would feel at home among his belongings. Custom, too, stated that a "spirit" would "go after" whoever disturbed its grave site.

"My grandaunt died an' they give us [Mrs. Jenkins, her sisters and brother] all her things: broom, bucket, dipper an' a rockin' chair. So that night [after the burial], she came in the house an' she played with everything that they give us. An' she did that all night!" The rocking chair creaked, the water dipper clanged against the metal bucket, and the broom's sweeping sounds spooked the listeners' ears until morning, Mrs. Jenkins testifies.

Another custom witnessed on St. Helena Island was the placing of a dollar bill in the first grave of a cemetery before the casket was lowered. The action was to "pay the ground" for receiving the dead. And a deceased person's family members younger than age six were passed once back and forth over the opened casket to keep the dead person's spirit from bothering them.

Because it was believed that the spirits of the dead roamed about, particularly in graveyards, cemeteries were shunned as much as possible.

Mrs. Jenkins begins another tale:
"One day we went in the graveyard to get some hick'ry nuts. An' while we was there getting those nuts, we heard these footsteps! We listen for a while . . . but after we didn't hear them again, we didn't think anything about it.

"When we hear it again, it was right up on us! We then turn and run, but we remember what our dad use to say: 'If anything scare you an' you run, make sure you don't fall. Because if you do an' that thing stop over you, you will die!'

"So I don't think any one of us fall — because every one of us is still here today!"

Another traditional bogey, the hag, still haunts the minds of those who believe in it. Whenever a person is awakened at night, feeling smothered and weighted

97

on his face and chest, being unable to sleep soundly or awaken completely, and knowing, frighteningly, that his screams are inaudible — even to himself, it is said that he is being "ridden" by a hag.

A hag, supposedly, straddles an individual's face and "rides" him, causing disorientation and panic. Unbelievers say that the state of being hag-ridden arises from poor blood circulation, nervousness, or excessive worrying.

Tale bearers, though, declare that hags are ordinary community members who are empowered to shed their human skins, change their forms or become invisible, and torment others by "riding" them. One could rid himself of a hag by throwing salt at it (in which case it could not return to its human skin and, consequently, would die) or by cursing at it vehemently. Others prayed. Babies were protected by placing match sticks in their hair.

Embellishments of the belief include:

A hag sucked the blood out of an individual and sold it for profit; hence, if a supposedly poor neighbor spoke frequently about visits to distant places, he or she was labeled a "hag."

A hag was any elderly community member who wanted to get back at someone who had wronged or annoyed him or her.

If a broom was placed near the doorway, a hag, even in its human form, would not enter one's house.

Lending meaning to the past,
Nurturing strength and hope
For the future.

"Well, I come this far, fin' no fault, feel like journey on."

"HAPPY NEW YEAR! HAPPY NEW YEAR!"

The greeting, proclaimed with jubilation, is exchanged with smiles, handshakes and embraces. For the last two hours, the Islanders have engaged in Watch Night Service: a traditional ceremony held since Reconstruction, in which Low-Country blacks greet the new year on their knees in prayer.

Watch Night Services initially were held in the plantation prayer houses. Beginning at 10 p.m. on New Year's Eve, Islanders assembled to sing rousing spirituals, pray and testify until five minutes before midnight. Doing the Shout would highlight the ceremony.

The Shout was not a vocal response, but a way of praising the Lord with the feet. Everyone would do the Shout, glorifying God for what He had done for them during the year. People would encircle the room, singing a spiritual until they had set the song. Then the beat would quicken. An excitement, a spiritual fervor would begin to move within their bodies. The people clapped their hands. Soon, their praises migrated to their feet. They would Shout!

The Shout was like doing the Charleston. But the feet were never crossed, which would signify worldly dancing. Instead, they were moved sprightly to either side. Shouting songs included "Walk in Jerusalem," "A Bony," "I Looked down the Road and I Started" and "Jubilee."

Got a home in Jubilee!
Oh, Lawd, Jubilee!
Yes, Lawd, Jubilee!
Thank God, Jubilee!

Sun da rise in Jubilee!
Oh, Lawd, Jubilee!
Yes, Lawd, Jubilee!
Thank God, Jubilee!

Goin' home to Jubilee!
Oh, Lawd, Jubilee!
Yes, Lawd, Jubilee!
Thank God, Jubilee!

With their singing, testifying and praising, the Islanders rejoice until five minutes before midnight. Then all the lights in the church building are turned off. The congregation kneels in silent prayer.

Four men called "travelers" assemble in each corner of the building. Alternately, each traveler sings this request to a leader at the front of the room: "Watchman, watchman, tell me the hour of the night."

101

The "watchman," in turn, states the time in song, concluding that all is well. At midnight, he proclaims: "Traveler, traveler, traveler — it is twelve o'clock, and all is well. HAPPY NEW YEAR!"

As the members rise to their feet, the lights are turned on. Eyes are alight with reverence as the Islanders reflect on God's goodness throughout the past year. Their eyes, too, are aglow with marvel as they greet neighbors and friends. For they have come this far. They will journey on.

"We got the gold. The gold is here. We just got to stoop down and pick it up!"

Melvin Gadsden exhorts the value of self-determination: "If the black man could see for himself, he wouldn't need [be economically dependent upon] the white man. The white man won't buy anything from you unless you have something to offer.

"But we got nothing to offer — but our labor. And the white man gives you just what he feels like for your labor. An' you have to take it or leave it!"

"Trouble will be over," however, a spiritual proclaims. To Gadsden, a portion of the answer is the land. For the land is gold.

"On St. Helena, black people could be the richest people in the world. But they give their land away for a little bit of money. Then the white man got you. If he say, 'Move!' you have to move — just like in slavery time."

He sorely remembers advising, pleading with and preaching to neighboring Coosaw Island blacks not to sell their land in recent years.

"But they was giving their land away. By the time they saw the value of it, it was too late. If they had a hundred or a thousand acres now, they could sell it and make a lot of money. They think that if they don't work for the white man, they can't make it. But it rains in your field just like it does in the white man's field. Black people need to do something for themselves!"

Gadsden advocates that landowners raise crops to defray expenses of buying products.

"They [are] in the country — raise food: peas, potatoes, watermelons, cucumbers, squash. Or they can plant peach trees, pear trees, fig trees, or pine. Or raise cattle. The gold is here! We just got to stoop down and pick it up."

A retired carpenter of forty-eight years, Gadsden prides himself in having built his own six-room house.

"God helps men that try to help themselves. The problem facing the black man is that he doesn't want to help himself. He's always looking for the white man to open up something for him. And some blacks are only concerned about self. They're too narrow-hearted."

The land — the St. Helena Islander's "gold," as Gadsden asserts — is quickly changing hands. Land developers for tourist and resort communities are continually acquiring huge areas of land. The concept and "flavoring" of the South Carolina "Sea Islands" soon may be changed to the "Resort Islands."

"There's a lack of good leadership," Gadsden adds. "A man that would think well of himself and of others would be a great help to his community."

Saint Helena Hymn

Oh, none in all the world before
    Were ever glad as we!
We're free on Carolina's shore,
    We're all at home and free.

(Saint Helena Hymn was written by John Greenleaf Whittier upon the request of
Charlotte Forten, first black instructor at Penn School. It was first sung on the Island
at Brick Baptist Church on Christmas Day 1862.)

Thou Friend and Helper of the poor,
    Who suffered for our sake,
To open every prison door,
    And every yoke to break!

Bend low Thy pitying face and mild,
    And help us sing and pray;
The hand that blessed the little child,
    Upon our foreheads lay.

We hear no more the driver's horn,
  No more the whip we fear,
This holy day that saw Thee born
  Was never half so dear.

The very oaks are greener clad,
    The waters brighter smile;
Oh, never shone a day so glad
    On sweet St. Helena's Isle.

We praise Thee in our songs today,
    To Thee in prayer we call,
Make swift the feet and straight the way
    Of freedom unto all.

Come once again, O blessed Lord!
    Come walking on the sea!
And let the mainlands hear the word
    That sets the island free!

The Author

Ronald Daise is a native of St. Helena Island, South Carolina, and was educated in the Beaufort County public school system. The last of nine children, he was born to Henry and Kathleen Grant Daise, both graduates of Penn School.

In 1978, Daise received a bachelor of arts degree in mass media arts, graduating with highest honors from Hampton Institute, now known as Hampton University in Hampton, Virginia. He worked as a newspaper reporter and features writer for *The Beaufort Gazette* after returning to Beaufort County and continues to work in the field of communications. Daise is a member of the Sea Island Translation Team, a volunteer group engaged in translating the Bible into Gullah. He and his wife, Natalie, have performed ''Sea Island Montage,'' a concert of songs, story-telling, sing-alongs and slides of information from this book, at colleges, schools, and cultural centers.

In addition to writing, his interests include performing, songwriting and singing. He aspires to record contemporary Christian music.

Ronald Daise and his wife reside in Beaufort, South Carolina.

Clarence L. Holte

Clarence L. Holte, of New York City, is the former contemporary bibliophile of the history and culture of black people. Named after him are: the International Clarence L. Holte Literary Prize (administered by the Schomburg Center for Research in Black Culture, New York City), the Clarence L. Holte Lectureship at Lincoln University, and the Clarence L. Holte Collection of Africana (Zaria, Nigeria).